COOPERATIVE LEARNING
An Effective Teaching Manual

June Belcher-Veasley

ENTEGRITY
CHOICE PUBLISHING

Entegrity Choice Publishing
PO Box 453
Powder Springs, GA 30127
info@entegritypublishing.com
www.entegritypublishing.com
770.727.6517

Printed in the United States of America

The views expressed in this work are solely those of the author and do not necessarily reflect the views of the publisher, and the publisher hereby disclaims any responsibility for them.

The publisher is not responsible for websites (or their content) that are not owned by the publisher.

Library of Congress Cataloging-in-Publication Data
ISBN 978-1-7325767-8-0
Library of Congress 2019941627

*A big thank you to all of the people who helped me begin and complete this body of work. I especially would like to thank **Mrs. Royce Love-Diagne** who was my back bone and inspirational guru. She kept me focused and on point during the building of this work. I hope this body of work will assist others who are called to teach.*

CONTENTS

CHAPTER I

Cooperative Learning...

Without the cooperation of its members,
society cannot survive and the society of man has
survived because the cooperativeness of its members…
It was not an advantageous individual here and there who
did so, but the group. In human society, the individuals who
are most likely to survive are those who are best enabled
to do so by their group.

~Ashely Montagu, 1965

INTRODUCTION

Atkinson (2001) coined the phase, "active learning is a WE thing, not a me thing. Always the product of many hands and heads." Atkinson's work supports the premise that working together to achieve a common goal produces higher achievement and greater productivity than working alone. Further support comes from the results of over 375 studies conducted over the past 100 years, which attest to the effectiveness of cooperative learning (Johnson & Johnson, 1989).

As a categorized group of instructional strategies, cooperative learning has been around for over 50 years and is still effective in helping students develop high academic success, positive self-esteem, inter-group relationships, and leadership skills (Salvin, 1995). Additionally, research has also demonstrated that cooperative learning leads to higher levels of academic achievement in children than direct instructional methods (Salvin, 1995).

Considering the research which supports cooperative learning as an effective instructional method, one might be curious as to the reasons why some educators are not knowledgeable of cooperative learning techniques. Unfortunately, however, during this study, direct observation revealed that effective implementation of cooperative learning techniques has been hindered in instances where teachers lacked sufficient knowledge about the benefits and mechanics of using cooperative grouping strategies to facilitate high levels of achievement.

This guide, however, is intended to serve as a cooperative learning strategy "blue print" or resource for teachers who desire to help young learners comprehend, grasp complex concepts, effectively communicate, collaborate, and ultimately experience high levels of academic success!

STATEMENT OF THE PROBLEM

The purpose of the study was to initially research and gather information on a variety of cooperative learning strategies which would subsequently be used to create a cooperative learning strategy implementation resource guide for teachers. The major focus of the guide address the following:

1. The cooperative learning concept and application
2. Specific descriptions and explanations of selected cooperative learning strategies
3. Explanation and guidelines for implementing cooperative learning activities
4. List of cooperative Learning Resources (books, articles, web sites)

LIMITATION AND DELIMITATION

Prior to beginning the masters program at Central Michigan University, the researcher had completed 20 years as an elementary and middle school teacher of at-risk students in grades 3-8. On numerous occasions, the researcher observed situations wherein teachers (and students) expressed disappointment and frustration with the level of comprehension and retention yielded by direct instruction teaching methods.

Consequently, motivated by the desire to provide frustrated teachers with new and innovative instructional strategies, the researcher sought to fully comprehend the cooperative learning concept and related activities. This guide is the product of an exhaustive research effort. It is intended to be used by Elementary school teachers and other stakeholders who desire to provide effective, interesting learning opportunities for students.

DEFINITION OF TERMS

Effective - having the effect of producing an outcome.

Cooperative learning - the relationship amongst a group of students that requires positive interdependence (a sense of sink or swim together), individual accountability (each of us has to contribute and learn), interpersonal skills (communication, trust, leadership, decision making, and conflict resolution), face-to-face interaction, and processing (reflecting on how well the team is functioning and how to make it function better) (Johnson, 2001).

Method - refers to a way of doing something or strategy.

Positive interdependence - means that students must concern themselves with the performance of all members of the team, not only with their own performance. (A team task must be structured and clearly stated, so that each teammate understands it.) (Johnson, 2001).

Individual accountability - the process of holding each member of the cooperative learning team accountable for the performance of the team. Each team member must be able to report the results of the team's work and be able to explain how the team obtained its results. (Johnson, 2001).

Heterogeneous - the combination of unrelated or different elements or parts (i.e., girls and boys of varying intellects, etc.). In cooperative learning, teams are made up of heterogeneous interns of ability, gender, ethnicity, and other personal characteristics (Johnson, 2001).

Shared leadership - the process through which each member of the team shares leadership responsibilities. The team has no formal leader. Instead, each member of the team has a job to do.

Partnership in a team - students focus on both the content and skills aspects of academic assignments. They focus on the need for working together. They review the success of the assignment and how well they cooperated with each other. They try to improve both their academic learning and their ability to cooperate (Johnson, 2001).

Social skills -the ability to communicate and work cooperatively with peers in an effort to complete a task or achieve a goal.

Teacher as the consultant – the act of providing feedback to the teams relative to how effectively or ineffectively team members work together and suggestions relative to ways that answers can be obtained or improvements made.

Trust building - the act of showing respect for one another's ideas and constructive criticism and suggestions.

SUMMARY

Cooperative learning is a tried and true instructional strategy. It can be used to facilitate high levels of academic achievement. Cooperative learning can also be used to help students develop and achieve a sense of positive interdependence, individual accountability, interpersonal, critical thinking, and processing skills (Johnson, 2001). A guide has been developed in an effort to provide teachers and other stakeholders with cooperative learning activities.

CHAPTER II
A REVIEW OF
RELATED LITERATURE

INTRODUCTION

The researcher conducted an extensive research of related literature and resources accessible via the ERIC electronic research system. The research completed in this chapter focused on the impact that teachers had in the development and implementation of cooperative learning strategies. Specifically, it examined the ways that teachers used cooperative learning as a strategy for facilitating increased academic achievement.

According to Atkinson, using effective grouping models in the classroom can aid teachers in a variety of ways. Some are as follows:

- Students develop interpersonal skills which help to reduce the frequency of unresolved conflicts and or disagreements.
- Teachers experience a reduction in the amount of stress that they endure while trying to answer large volumes of individual student questions. Through cooperative learning, students work cooperatively to solve problems and ask questions collectively.
- Students use positive peer pressure to inculcate a productive work ethic amongst group members, etc.

By using a myriad of cooperative learning strategies and activities, the teacher will be able to facilitate higher levels of academic achievement.

REVIEW OF RELATED LITERATURE

According to Wittrock (1990), educators have for many years encouraged teachers to use cooperative groups in the classroom. Teachers who used cooperative learning strategies in the classroom helped to develop high academic achievement among their students.

This study showed that students learned and retained more information when they worked collaboratively than when they worked alone. The literature review found numerous references that also supported the effective use of cooperative learning in the classroom.

Several studies were conducted wherein it was found that, "when children worked cooperatively, they develop an understanding of the unanimity of purpose of the group of the need to help and support each other's learning (Sharn & Shaulov, 1990)." Literature also supports the premise that when children work in cooperative groups, they develop language that is more inclusive; they become consistently more cooperative and helpful.

Most cooperative learning research has focused on the effects of cooperative learning groups on students (Johnson & Johnson, 1998; Salvin, 1991, p. 6). Studies have examined student achievement, cognitive skills, social skills, self-esteem, and cross-cultural relationships. They have concluded that cooperative learning models are more effective when used with urban learners. Especially in the cases where the learners are considered to be academically deficient, cooperative learning has helped students to experience academic success in small group settings. They become more interactive, social, and responsible for their learning.

According to Siciliano (2001), the cooperative learning framework has five elements or principles: (a) positive interdependence, (b) face–to–face (positive) interaction, (c) individual accountability, (d) social skills, and (e) group processing. This framework was developed to improve the team process. Specifically, it was designed to keep student attention focused on assigned tasks and to provide incentives for students to assist one another in understanding the concepts or theories.

According to Gillies and Ashman (1997), when children of different abilities (high, medium, and low) were trained to work together in heterogeneous ability groups (high/medium/low), they were consistently more cooperative and productive. They provided more helpful explanations and assistance to their peers than those in the untrained group. Moreover, the children in the trained groups attained higher learning outcomes than their peers in the untrained or control groups.

Research states that cooperative learning is a teaching strategy in which students work together in small teams and use a number of activities to achieve academic objectives and improve their understating of subject matter. Using a collaborative group structure, teachers encourage interdependency among group members while assisting students to work together in small groups so that all participate in the sharing of data and in developing group reports (National Research Council, 1996).

According to Chang & Barufaldi (1999), a cooperative learning course of study is more effective in enhancing a higher cognitive domain than more traditional teaching methods.

In fact, Berger & Thompson (1995) found that cooperative learning is an increasingly popular way to organize lessons. This method is based on the assumption that groups of people who can work together will be the key to success in the emerging global marketplace. Educators believe that in order to acquire the social skills necessary for this environment, students should begin working in teams as early as possible. By early adolescence, students are ready for learning in teams because egocentrism declines, they prefer to be with peers, and they can demonstrate a capacity to use critical thinking as well as introspection.

Researcher Vygotsky (1978) stated that collaborative activity amongst children's proximal zones of development is more advanced than those that they could perform as individuals. He also stated that the influence of collaborative activity on learning is as follows:

"Functions are first formed in the collective as relations among children and then become mental functions for the individual."

Similarly, Piaget (1926) held that social-arbitrary knowledge – language, values, rules, morality, and symbol systems – could only be learned in interactions with others.

On the basis of these and other findings, many Piagetians have called for an increase in the use of cooperative activities in schools. It is argued that interactions amongst students on learning tasks will lead to improved student achievement. It is further believed that students will learn more from one another in their discussions of the content.

Cognitive conflict will also arise, inadequate reasoning will be exposed, disequilibration will occur, and higher–quality understandings will emerge. He further goes on to say that the effects of cooperative learning on student achievement would be largely or entirely due to the use of cooperative tasks. In this view, the opportunity for students to discuss, to argue, to present, and hear one another's viewpoints is the critical element of cooperative learning.

For Example, Damon (1984) integrates Piagetian, Vygotskian, and Sullivanian perspectives on peer collaboration to propose a "conceptual foundation for a peer-based plan of education," which is as follows:

1. Through mutual feedback and debate, peers motivate each other to abandon misconceptions and search for better solutions.
2. The experience of peer communication can help a child master social processes such as participation, argumentation, and cognitive processes like verification and criticism.
3. Collaboration between peers can provide a forum for discovery learning and can encourage creative thinking.
4. Peer interaction can introduce children to the process of generating ideas.

According to Salvin (1995), it is believed that research supports the fact that cooperative learning strongly supports the importance of group goals that can be achieved only by ensuring the learning of all group members.

Researchers Johnson & Johnson (1989) also support the same conclusions that when students learn together, all group members benefit.

Cooperative learning is one of the most innovative and instructional methods in the history of educational research. While there was research on this topic dating back to the earliest days of this century, the amount and quality of the research greatly accelerated in the early 1970s and continues unabated today, a quarter-century later! Hundreds of studies have compared the most frequent objectives of this research to determine the effects of cooperative learning on student achievement. Studies of the achievement effects of cooperative learning have taken place in every major subject area. Further, cooperative learning is not only a subject of research and theory; it is used at some level by millions of teachers. A recent national survey by researchers Puma, Jones, Rock, & Fernandez (1993) found that 79% of elementary teachers and 62% of middle school teachers reported sustained use of cooperative learning strategies.

SUMMARY

There is an abundance of information including journal articles that discuss the effectiveness of using cooperative learning strategies in the classroom. Additionally, it has been found that teachers who have incorporated cooperative learning strategies have found that their students experienced high levels of academic success. The literature supports the belief that constant teacher use of cooperative learning can help students achieve success.

CHAPTER III
HANDBOOK

INTRODUCTION TO PRODUCT

The major goal of this guide is to encourage teachers to use cooperative learning as an instructional method which addresses the instructional needs of learners with a variety of modalities. The belief is that cooperative learning will enhance academic achievement. The primary focus of this guide is to help the teacher with comprehending and implementing cooperative learning strategies in the classroom so that a higher level of academic achievement can be attained.

With continuous guidance from educators and researchers who are proficient in implementing cooperative learning strategies, teachers will continue to receive a plethora of ideas, strategies, and methods that will enhance the academic achievement of learners. Additionally, through the use of cooperative learning, teachers will be encouraged to interact with other teachers and educational stakeholders in the development of new cooperative learning strategies.

Furthermore, this guide is a resource which provides tips, suggestions, web sites, and additional resources relative to effective implementation of cooperative learning strategies. Several publications were used in the development and organization of this guide.

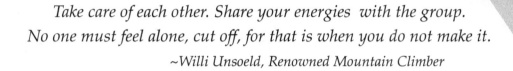

Take care of each other. Share your energies with the group.
No one must feel alone, cut off, for that is when you do not make it.
~Willi Unsoeld, Renowned Mountain Climber

The cooperative learning handbook was created to be a skill-oriented handbook that facilitates the effective implementation of cooperative strategies. It was also designed to encourage students to work together in cooperative groups to develop and master the following:

1. Problem-solving techniques
2. Decision-making strategies
3. Enhanced communication skills and positive self-esteem
4. Interdependence (during group interaction)

The guide provides cooperative learning activities that emphasize positive interdependence among group members and the sharing of goals with individual accountability. Many activities are for developing small group skills and the processing of ideas as well as face-to-face interaction. The pages in this guide are reproducible and can be used as a template for designing specialized cooperative group projects and assignments.

The information in this guide has been presented in four parts, which include information on the following: conceptual framework, strategies, activities, and resources.

DEFINITION OF TERMS

Conceptual – existing or dealing with what exists only in the mind.

Folktales – a story that is passed down from generation to generation that teaches a lesson or has a moral.

Guidelines – a set of rules governing the completion of the activity or assigned task.

Interaction – to communicate with one another in a manner that will lead to project completion.

Learning Style – the way in which one learns.

Strategy – a way of doing something, method, manner.

A CONCEPTUAL VIEW
OF COOPERATIVE LEARNING

Robert J. Stahl and Ronald L. Vansickle (1997) p. 3, state that in order for teachers to use appropriately cooperative learning methods, they must have an adequate conceptual view of cooperation and cooperative learning. They further go on to say that when cooperative learning is used in the classroom for a sufficient period of time, both the quantity and the quality of interaction are high and student achievement for all is optimal for the time spent on task.

Salvin (1983) goes on to say that teachers need to establish heterogeneous groups of four to six members who are mutually responsible for each other's success relative to the same knowledge and abilities.

As stated by Johnson, Johnson, and Holubec (1990), p. 3, the cooperative learning framework should modify misconceptions about cooperative learning and help to prevent future misconceptions from arising. The researchers go on to present ideas that should become permanent attributes of the cooperative learning concept. The attributes are as follows:

1. Not all-cooperative groups are instructionally effective (Salvin, 1990). Educators must understand that only the groups which meet established guidelines and standards can be considered cooperative learning groups.

2. Cooperative learning does not oppose all forms of academic competition. However, in order for cooperative groups to be effective, students must come to envision their group as a non-competitive, united team. The team must then embrace the

mutually beneficial goals of achieving success for the group and individual members.

3. Cooperative learning strategies should not replace all other teaching strategies in the classroom but must be viewed as an alternative approach to structuring teaching and learning tasks. Co-operative learning can also lead to student involvement in competitive situations. It can develop skills that challenge students to engage in competition and experience the fun associated with pursuit and rivalry (Johnson et.al, 1984). Co-operative learning groups can take on many forms, all of which require that students work interdependently in small groups to help each other acquire and retain the academic content and skills established for them.

4. Cooperative learning approaches are instructional guides. Cooperative learning strategies are strategies for structuring the learning environment within classrooms. These strategies are tools that facilitate student progress toward achieving the cognitive affective and social outcomes set within the curriculum used. These strategies are to be used after the curriculum decisions have been made.

5. Cooperative learning strategies are independent of the outcomes selected and the materials used during the group tasks (Stahl 1990). Teachers may use many cooperative learning strategies in connection with textbooks, content-filled handouts, or other printed resources that are aligned with students learning. Every cooperative learning strategy, when used appropriately, can enable students to move beyond the text, memorization of basic facts, and learning lower-level skills. Students become proficient transferees of academic and social knowledge and abilities.

6. Cooperative learning techniques or strategies are structured ways of operating within a classroom. One key for ensuring that cooperative learning strategies work is to envision each strategy as describing a particular way to structure the learning, the learning task, and the

learner's roles (Kagan, 1989, 1989-90). Such structures are content–free ways of organizing social interaction aimed toward enabling all students to be successful. Structures provide steps, guidelines, and requirements that, when met, will allow students to achieve their maximum potential in alignment with clear outcomes. Teachers may use structures such as Jigsaw, Co-op, Co-op, and Teams–Games–Tournament over and over across an extremely wide range of topics, content, grade levels, and outcomes (Kagan, 1989, 1989–90). The structures differ according to their cognitive processing; academic, affective, and interpersonal emphasis; length of time for completion; required teacher and student roles; and usefulness for selected content and degree of complexity.

7. Each cooperative learning strategy should be viewed as a structural way of operating within the classroom. When operating within a group, the students or the teacher must ensure that they are meeting requirements for appropriate cooperative learning group work. What counts as a cooperative learning task(s) and environment should be structured so that the requirements are met. When students complete appropriate cooperative tasks, teachers find that large numbers of students leave the group tasks and the course with high levels of success for the outcomes set for them.

8. Each group member needs to learn appropriate cooperative group behaviors. Students must acquire, practice, and refine the variety of positive group behaviors necessary for them to work as a group so that they become skilled users of these abilities and accompanying attitudes. Teachers will need to take time before they form the groups, during the group interactions, and after the groups have finished, to describe particular productive and dysfunctional group behaviors and attitudes. This is as much a part of the group learning process as the academic content and abilities. Proponents of cooperative learning emphasize the need to help students learn what is necessary to contribute to the group's goal–directed efforts.

9. Appropriate cooperative learning structures and guidelines are neither simple nor easy to implement (Johnson et. al, 1984). Even for teachers who have used groups in the past, learning concepts and procedures of cooperative strategies and properly implementing them in the classroom require time, effort, and adherence to the criteria provided. Cooperative learning as an approach to teaching generally and the various cooperative strategies in particular are complex ways of operating in the classroom. They require the teacher to use a number of new behaviors that will take time to perfect. Teachers who use cooperative learning strategies must keep in mind that cooperation among instructors and students will impact how much they are willing to accept the fact that creating an effective cooperative learning classroom will be at time tedious and challenging work. Persistence and constant usage will result in positive results for both the students and the teachers and make the effort of using cooperative learning worthwhile (Johnson et al., 1984).

10. And finally, cooperative learning will work when only one teacher in the school is using it. Cooperative learning has been effective in achieving many of the valued goals of education. With the consistent use of cooperative learning, teachers can expect to achieve academic success in the classroom.

In conclusion, these concepts address a number of appropriate cooperative learning fundamentals to consider when using cooperative learning strategies in the classroom. These ideas should be included as a part of a large, comprehensive, conceptual framework for cooperative learning.

COOPERATIVE LEARNING GUIDELINES AND REQUIREMENTS

Teachers who use groups must keep in mind that in order to use cooperative learning strategies appropriately, they must recognize that the cooperative learning strategies are more effective if a certain number of guidelines are met (e.g., Aronson et al., 1978, Cohen, 1989, Johnson & Johnson, 1991, Johnson et al., 1984, Kagan, 1989, Salvin, 1983, 1990, Stahl, 1992). One way to determine whether cooperative learning is occurring is to observe how closely students follow the structures and requirements, keeping in mind that group members must meet requirements if cooperative activity is occurring. For instance, most students involved in cooperative learning over an extended period of time should show evidence of the following:

- Improved academic test scores.
- Increased and meaningful interaction with peers.
- Strong feelings of inclusion and group membership.
- Increased willingness to work cooperatively in small group settings and achieve common goals.
- Positive attitudes necessary for working effectively with others.
- Integration of their academic learning and social inter-group relations.
- Improved relationship between individuals from diverse ethnic or racial groups.
- Willingness to express and discuss ideas in public.
- Improved opinions about relationships with disabled students.
- Positive self–concept and self–esteem.
- Positive psychological adjustment.

- Increase in intrinsic motivation.
- Acceptance of peers as knowledge partners in learning and as resources.
- Proficiency in the use of critical thinking strategies.
- Reduction in disruptive behavior.
- Increased time they spent on-task.
- Positive attitudes toward teachers, principals, and other school personnel.
- Positive attitudes toward learning, school, and the subject matter content.

Teachers must keep in mind that the cooperative learning groups, whether lasting one class period, one week, or one month, will not generate all of these results every time, but rather these results are likely to occur when learning groups function over an extended period of time. Taking and using these guidelines will ensure that teachers and students will work collaboratively and cooperatively to increase the effectiveness of cooperative learning groups in the classrooms. (Stahl, & Vansickle, 1997).

USING COOPERATIVE LEARNING STRATEGIES PROVIDE STUDENTS WITH WHAT THEY NEED TO KNOW

According to Stahl & VanSickle, (1997), cooperative learning strategies provide students with many opportunities to gain access to the information they need, to complete the processing they need to complete, and to spend extended on–task time learning in direct alignment with the goals selected. Research shows that using cooperative groups serves to enhance the student's achievement ability in the following ways:

a) Increases the relevant information that would otherwise be available to a single person.
b) Provides and supports alternative versions and perspectives of what they are studying.
c) Helps students complete appropriate internal information processing.
d) Increases the use of self–regulatory abilities to stay focused.
e) Monitors student's thinking and actions such that correction and reinforcement will be more immediate, frequent, and constructive.
f) Verifies students' ideas and abilities within moments after being expressed.

Therefore, when students work as groups to facilitate each other's learning, each student has engaged time to learn information and abilities associated with the goals.

COOPERATIVE LEARNING STRATEGIES

According to Salvin (1978,1986), dozens of specific cooperative learning strategies are available with teachers' manuals or other how–to materials; hundreds of informal variations of these are available as well. The small number of strategies that have been empirically compared to traditionally taught control groups and applied in the education arena are described below.

Student's Teams – Achievement Divisions

In STAD (Salvin, 1978, 1986), teachers assign students to four–member teams that are mixed by performance level, gender, and ethnicity. The teacher first presents a lesson, and then students work within their teams to make sure that all team members have learned the lesson. Finally, all students take individual quizzes on the material without helping one another.

Next, the teacher compares students' quiz scores to their past averages and awards points based on the degree to which students can meet or exceed their earlier individual performances. The teacher then adds their points to form their scores. Teams that meet certain reestablished criteria may earn certificates or other rewards. The whole cycle of activities, from the teacher presentation to team practice to quiz, usually takes three to five class periods.

STAD has been used in a wide variety of subjects from mathematics to language arts to social studies and has been used from grade 2 through college. It is most appropriate for teaching well–defined objectives with single right answers, such as specific locations in geography and some map skills, knowledge of events in history, and principles of economics or government.

According to the Salmon River–GLC Eisenhower Project (2001), STAD had five major components: class presentations, teams, quizzes, individual improvement scores, and team recognition. STAD is one of the simplest of all cooperative learning strategies and is a good strategy to begin with for the teachers who are new to the cooperative approach. *(See Appendixes)*

Wordsplash

A Wordsplash is a collection of key terms or concepts taken from a written passage (a chapter of a textbook or a newspaper or magazine article) which the students are about to read. The terms selected represent important ideas that the teacher wants the students to attend to when they actually do the reading later, but initially the students' tasks is to make predictive statements about how each of the terms relates to the title or main focus of the reading. Most terms selected for a Wordsplash are familiar vocabulary for students. The novelty of the terms is only the way in which the terms are associated with the new topic.

Display selected terms randomly and at angles on a visual (overhead or chart). Students brainstorm and generate complete statements (not just words or phrases) which predict the relationship between each term and the broader topic. Once students have generated statements for each term, they turn to the printed material, read it to check the accuracy of their predictive statements, and revise where needed. When students have read and revised their predictions, encourage them to quiz each other on the correct information, Salmon River – GLC Eisenhower Project (2001). *(See Appendixes)*

Teams–Games Tournament

Teams–Games–Tournament (DeVries and Salvin, 1978; Salvin, 1986) was the first of the Johns Hopkins cooperative learning methods. It uses the same teacher presentation and teamwork as STAD but replaces the quizzes with weekly tournaments in which students compete with members of other teams to contribute points to their own team scores.

Jigsaw

Elliot, Aronson, and his colleagues (1978} originally designed Jigsaw. According to Aronson's Jigsaw method, teachers assign students to six–member teams to work on academic material that the teacher has broken down into sections. For example, a biography might be divided into early life, first accomplishment, major set-back, later life, and influences on history. Each team member reads an assigned section. Next, members of different teams who have studied the same sections meet in expert groups to discuss their sections. Then students return to their original teams and take turns teaching their teammates about their respective sections of the material. Since the only way students can learn other sections is to listen carefully to their teammates, they are motivated to support and show interest in one another's work.

In Salvin's (1986) modification of Jigsaw, Jigsaw II, students work in four or five-member teams as in TGT and STAD. Instead of each student being assigned a unique section, all students read a common narrative, such as a book chapter, a short story, or a biography. Each student then receives a subtopic related to this narrative on which to become an expert. Students with the same topics meet in expert groups to discuss them, after which they return to their original teams to teach what they have learned to their teammates. Students then take individual quizzes, which result in team scores based on the improvement score system of STAD. Teams that meet preset standards may earn certificates or other suitable rewards. Kagan (1989) has described many more variations of the basic Jigsaw format.

Learning Together
Group Investigation
Research on Academic Achievement
Inter-group Relations
Mainstreaming

According to the Salmon River – GLC Eisenhower Project (2001), the Jigsaw is also a flexible way of structuring positive interdependence among group members, and teachers have developed many variations. Here are several modifications that are helpful in different circumstances:

1. Give students subtopics and have them use reference materials in the library to research their subtopic. This frees the teacher from having to arrange materials in advance.
2. Have the group write a report or give a class presentation on the overall topic, with the specification that it includes all the subtopics presented in the group.
3. Prepare outlines or study guides of what each subtopic should cover and have students read the same text, organizing and becoming experts on the material highlighted by their outline or study guide.
4. Distribute a set of reading materials or problems to each group. The set needs to be divisible into the number of members of the group (2, 3, or 4 parts). Give each member one part of the set of materials.
5. Allow individual students sufficient time to review or work on their assigned material and become an expert on it. You may assign them the cooperative task of meeting with someone else in the class who is a member of another learning group and who has the same section to prepare. Both of them need to help each other plan how to teach the material or explain their problem solving to the other members of their original cooperative groups.
6. Assign students the cooperative task of meeting with someone else in the class or another preparation pair who have learned the same material to share ideas as to how the material may best be taught. These practice groups review what each plans to teach their group presentations.
7. Have students return to their original cooperative groups and assign them the cooperative tasks of teaching their area of expertise to the other group members and learning the material being taught by them.

8. Assess students' degree of mastery of all the material. Reward the groups whose members all reach the preset criterion of excellence or give bonus points on their individual scores if these criteria are met. Students will need to evaluate themselves on how well their group did in the Jigsaw (e.g., active listening, checking each other for understanding, and encouraging each other), and set goals for further interaction.

Self - Esteem

In conclusion, researchers Stahl and Vansickle (1987) state that cooperative learning in the classroom shows that these strategies have great potential for teaching a wide variety of topics while enhancing an even wider variety of social skills and pro-social attitudes. Putting students into groups and asking them to work together, however, is not enough. Positive social outcomes have been found for a wide variety of methods, but achievement gains appear to depend on the use of group goals and individual accountability. Group success must depend on the learning or performance of every student, not on a single group.

Roundtable

Roundtable is a technique used for brainstorming or reviewing. Groups are seated around a table with one pencil and one piece of paper. A question is posed, and students take turns recording answers on the paper as it is passed around the table. The question should be carefully chosen. It should have multiple answers, and students should be capable of answering it. When time is called, teams count their responses written on the paper. Answers are then shared and validated by the entire class. Teams should share their successful strategies before going on to another round. Variations complete answers (Salmon River - GLC Eisenhower Project, 2001).

Numbered Heads

Students are arranged in teams of three or four, and each individual is assigned a number. Groups are assigned a learning task and given time to accomplish the task. Everyone is encouraged to learn the material because one question is posed, and the number of a student is then called. This student is only one answer sheet when written assignments are completed collectively (Salmon River – GLC Eisenhower Project, 2001).

Talking Chips

This is a method of providing opportunities for all members of a group to participate in a discussion. In order to talk, a student must place a chip (a pen will do) in a central area. Students cannot talk a second time until pens from everyone are placed in the center. This technique assures that all students have an opportunity to comment on the topic (Salmon River – GLC Eisenhower Project, 2001).

Three Step Interview

Students that are grouped in fours first work in pairs. One student interviews or questions another. Students then switch roles with the interviewer becoming the one interviewed. Findings are shared among the group of four in a "round robin" fashion.

This technique may be used when introducing a new topic. Questions such as, "What do you already know?" "What do you want to learn?" and "How can we do this?" increase student awareness and motivation (Salmon River – GLC Eisenhower Project, 2001).

HOW COOPERATIVE LEARNING STRATEGIES WORK

According to Kagan (1988), cooperative learning is more than just having students work together; cooperative learning is a set of instructional strategies that include cooperative student-to-student interaction based on subject matter as an integral part of the learning process. Salvin (1987) concurs that individual accountability is important and adds group rewards and equal opportunities for success as key elements.

Through various styles of research it has been stated that cooperative learning differs from traditional group work in that it includes structuring of learning tasks and evaluation to ensure positive interdependence and individual accountability. Therefore, research has proven that there are numerous types of cooperative learning strategies. Some are designed for mastery of basic skills and information, while others are oriented toward complex group projects requiring higher level thinking skills. Although specifically designed curriculum materials are available for cooperative learning, there are models that provide frameworks for applying cooperative learning in any subject area and grade level using regular materials found in classrooms.

FACILITATION OF COOPERATIVE LEARNING

According to Hertz–Lazarowitz and Fuks (1987; Kroll, Masigila, and Mace (1992), teachers can use many methods to facilitate cooperative learning. Teachers must keep in mind that in designing a cooperative learning setting in the classroom, special attention is usually given to the following issues:

1) The structure of the cooperative groups
2) Students' interactions in each group
3) Interactions among the different groups
4) Learning tasks and the teacher's role in the classroom
5) Assessment and evaluation of the learning process

These five criteria influence the type of cooperative learning setting that takes place in the classroom and its success.

STEPS TO USING TWO POPULAR COOPERATIVE LEARNING STRATEGIES

Listed in the two charts is the implementation of two of the most popular cooperative learning strategies used in the classroom: Jigsaw and Co-op Co-op. These strategies used in cooperative learning will help to enhance the student academic success. Listed below is also an evaluation chart to help the learner as well as the facilitator to evaluate the usefulness of the strategies. Such an evaluation will allow for the facilitator to determine which groups are working together cohesively or which ones needs to be reevaluated and restructured for maximum effort.

JIGSAW

Overview	• The purpose of Jigsaw is to have a group of students teach each other factual content. • Each child is assigned to both a study group and a learning team. First, study groups meet and by studying together become expert on their assigned topic. Next, students go to their learning teams to teach teammates the content they have learned in the study group. • Finally, all students in the class are tested and held individually accountable for knowing the content presented by all learning team members.
Steps	1. Obtain or prepare curriculum materials so that each study group member has specific information to teach to his learning team. 2. Form teams in accordance with the guidelines. 3. Conduct team-building exercises as suggested. 4. Select and prepare study group leaders to keep their groups on task, resolve differences, and serve as contact persons with the teacher. 5. Assign each team member a number. 6. Have students report to their study groups according to their number. All of the "1s" will get together, etc. 7. Distribute materials to students. All of the "1s" receive the same materials. The "2s" receive identical materials different from those given to the "1s," etc. 8. Instruct each group to become expert in the content it has been given. Each study group teaches and tests each member until all members thoroughly understand the assigned content. 9. When the study group content has been mastered, students rejoin their learning teams. Each team member teaches his assigned content to the rest of the group and learns from the others the content they were assigned to teach. Learning teams teach and test members until maximum learning is achieved within the time limit. 10. Test all members of the class on all of the content. 11. Assign grades consisting of the average of each student's individual score and the team mean. For example, if Joe's individual score is 88 and the team mean is 84, then Joe receives test score of 86. 12. Inform students at the beginning of the activity that their grades will be partially dependent on the team mean. Realizing that their grades will be affected by the achievement of their teammates encourages students to stay on-task and minimizes socializing in the teams.

Barnes, Farrell (1988)

CO-OP CO-OP

Overview	• Co-op Co-op is a very broad and useful framework with a wide variety of contents. It is designed for small groups working together to further their own understanding which they then share with the whole class. The name Co-op Co-op is derived from this design; the students are cooperating in small groups in order to cooperate with the entire class. • The duration of Co-op Co-op units can vary from one-day mini-projects to units lasting several weeks. This approach can be used concurrently with a traditional class structure. In this example, students work one or two days a week on their Co-op Co-op projects.
Steps	1. Teams are formed. 2. Team building exercises are conducted as suggested. 3. The class is led in a student-centered discussion of the unit to be studies. The purpose of this discussion is to determine what the students want to learn during the unit, not to lead them to identify specific topics at this early stage of the unit. 4. Each team then selects a unit-related topic. In a unit on the Middle East, for example, one team might select Egyptian inventions, another imports-exports, etc. 5. Teams subdivide their topic among team members. Individual student choice is of high priority, but teacher approval is required. 6. Students research their subtopics using not only their texts, but also all other available information and materials. 7. Each student presents what was learned to the team. Team feedback is provided each presenter and suggestions made regarding the preparation of a presentation to the entire class. 8. Team members refine their presentations. 9. Team presentations are made to the entire class. The teacher encourages innovative formats (skits, AV, debates, and demonstrations). 10. Evaluation consists of: individual self-evaluations; team self-evaluations; class evaluations of the group presentation; and, teacher evaluation of individual and group work and presentations.(See sample evaluation forms.)

Barnes, Farrell (1988)

TEAM SELF-EVALUATION

Group Name _____ Date _____

Topic of Study _____

Please place a check in each column that applies to your group.
(To be completed by each team member)

	Usually	Sometimes	Never
Everyone in our group knew what to do.			
Every group member did his or her job.			
Group members helped one another.			
Group members shared materials.			
Every group member helped make group decisions.			
Our group used its time wisely.			
Time wisely.			

Barnes, Farrell (1988) (See Appendixes)

Group		Work		Presentation	
Name	Used Time Well	Shared	Listened	Presented Good Information	Interesting Information
1.					
2.					
3.					

Barnes, Farrell (1988) (See Appendixes)

THE STRUCTURE OF
THE COOPERATIVE GROUP

According to Hertz (1987), the structure of a cooperative learning group is defined by the number of students within a group and by the degree of heterogeneity of a group. Artz and Newman (1990), Davidson (1990a), Davidson (1990b), Salvin (1985), Webb (1985), Hert, Lazarowitz, and Fuks (1987), discuss that the number of the students in a group depends on the type of the activity that is intended to take place in the classroom. In general, four is the optimal number of members in a cooperative learning group.

Some researchers recommend that students work in pairs and emphasize that working in pairs facilitates active learning. Others suggest that a group of six students is the best group size for a cooperative learning setting. However, all the researchers agree that the number of students in a group should not exceed seven.

The exchange–of–knowledge learning setting in this article gives students an opportunity to work in pairs within a large group of four to six students.

HETEROGENEITY OF A COOPERATIVE GROUP

According to Davidson (1990b), heterogeneity of a small group is one of the most important issues when planning a cooperative setting. Students learn better in groups of different ability levels, which are heterogeneous groups [Davidson (1990a), Davidson (1990b), Salvin (1985)]. Researchers have also noted that students with high ability levels prefer to learn with students having similar ability level. They also found that at the same time, students who have learning difficulties prefer to cooperate with students who are able to help them while learning. They further go on to state that in the exchange work in homogenous groups–of–knowledge method, the small groups would vary according to the different stages of learning.

Researchers also go on to say that students who begin their learning in a small heterogeneous group have an unlimited level of academic achievement. These students are usually placed in classroom that allows them to academically flourish. But on the other hand students who are placed in a small homogenous group are limited in their goals, academic achievement and are usually placed in the same classroom based upon their similar ability.

STUDENTS' INTERACTIONS IN GROUPS

Sharan et al.(1980) states that one of the main purposes of cooperative learning classrooms is to promote task–related interactions by students. The researcher further goes on to say that the learning method facilitates students' interaction, for example, when students are required to switch roles. Students' interactions can also be enhanced by the nature of the task; for example, the specific task can call for an exchange of ideas. The types of interactions depend on the types of learning objectives. The learning objective can be determined for each student individually. Cooperative learning within the group then is mainly a means for achieving the objectives. However, the learning objective can be determined for the group as a whole, in which case cooperation is a necessary condition in the learning setting. In the exchange–of–knowledge setting, students are assigned both individual and group learning objectives.

INTERACTIONS AMONG DIFFERENT GROUPS

Sharan et al. (1980) states that interactions among the learning groups may not take place. Students may present the results of their group work to the other group, or they may finish their group work within the small group without communicating with members of the other groups. Sharan (1980) goes on to say that interactions between various groups may be facilitated by some sort of competition. He goes on to say that in the exchange of knowledge methods, students switch from one working group to another on an individual basis and no interactions among the groups take place in the classroom.

TYPES OF LEARNING TASKS AND THE TEACHER'S ROLE IN THE CLASSROOM

According to Sharan (1980), the one crucial point of any cooperative learning setting is the teacher's role in the classroom. The way in which the learning material is presented to the students and the way in which a teacher communicates with students during the group work influence students' learning interactions. In the exchange–of– knowledge setting, the teacher's role is to help students solve problems when they request help. The learning tasks are presented as worked–out examples. This design is intended to focus students' interactions on understanding these examples by explaining to each other what they already know and by solving new problems similar to the worked–out examples.

Essentials of Cooperative Learning

Johnson, Johnson, Holubec, & Ray (1984), state that if cooperative learning is to be effective, the following guidelines need to be kept in mind:

1. Each student in the group is dependent upon all other group members in order for the group goal to be reached.
2. Tasks are divided among group members.
3. Group members share material, resources, and information.
4. Each student in the class is dependent upon all members of all groups for learning.
5. Students must interact directly with one another.

6. Each student must be held accountable for mastering the material assigned to all groups.
7. Students must be taught the skills necessary for group functioning. These include listening, taking turns, offering ideas, asking questions, and compromising.

Working with Teams

Salvin (1987) states that there are two essential activities in working with cooperative learning teams. They are team formation and building team spirit: forming teams and team building exercises.

Forming Teams

Salvin states that forming team procedures have been found to be effective in establishing effective teams. These procedures are as follows:

1. Rank order of students according to achievement and how best they learn from highest to lowest.
2. Assign the top, bottom, and two middle achievers to team one.
3. Using the remaining students in the achievement list, repeat this process until all teams are formed.
4. Heterogeneous teams are essential to the success of cooperative learning.
5. Revise teams if:
   a) Members are all of the same sex.
   b) Teams do not proportionately reflex the ethnic makeup of the class.
   c) Best friends are on the same team.
   d) Students who have serious difficulty getting along are on the same team.

Teambuilding Exercises

Salvin, Barnes, & Farrell (1987) go on to state that team building is a key element of cooperative learning. It is important for members of a team to develop respect and trust for each other to provide a setting in which learning can be maximized. If team building is neglected, the group's members may be too competitive or too social.

Teams must develop a feeling of interdependency so that each person's gain is everyone's gain. Occasional competition between teams is fine, but the goal should be to develop a cooperative classroom where all students view themselves as being on the same side and encourage each other to do their best. An important advantage of team building is that these skills can be transferred to other activities. Following are suggested procedures for successful teambuilding:

1. Ask each team to choose a name, pennant, motto, or other identification symbol. Emphasize that all team members must be listened to. Decisions must be by consensus, not by majority vote, and no member is permitted to vote for something with which he seriously disagrees. These rules provide guides for future interactions, which require participation, consensus, and respect for individual rights.

2. Have teams engage in activities such as "Roundtable." This usually consists of having one piece of paper and one pen for each team. One student makes a written contribution and then passes the paper to the next team member. The teacher asks questions with many possible correct answers, such as name all the states you can or all the equivalent fractions for one-half. Roundtable can be used as a race or with little or no time pressure.

3. Have teams participate in trust-building exercises such as:
   a) Team members catch one member who falls backward. Emphasize safety procedures.

b) Team members guide a blindfolded member around obstacles in the room.

c) Teams put together a simple puzzle, which requires each member to contribute. Each member may be given several pieces of the puzzle to foster participation and interdependence (Salvin, 1987).

Group Roles

According to Salvin (1987), in order for cooperative groups to be successful, each group member must have an active part in which they help to make the group a more cooperative or successful one. Listed below are group roles for cooperative learning groups:

- **Summarizer** - restates the group's major conclusion or answers.
- **Checker of Understanding** - ensures that all group members can explicitly explain how to arrive at an answer or conclusion.
- **Accuracy Coach** - corrects any mistakes in another member's explanations or summaries.
- **Elaborator** - relates current concepts and strategies to materials studied previously.
- **Research** - Runner: gets needed materials for the group and communicates with the other learning groups and the teacher.
- **Recorder** - writes down the group's decisions and edits the group's report.
- **Encourager of Participation** - ensures that all members are contributing.
- **Observer** - keeps track of how well the group is cooperating.
- **Time–Keeper** - makes sure that tasks are accomplished on time; keep the group aware of the amount of time to work in.
- **Praiser** - praises good ideas; helps members feel good about their contributions.
- **Encourager** - asks silent members what they think or what they can add; listens to others in a way that encourages them to speak.

- **Harmonizer** - attempts to settle disagreements; reduces tension; seeks compromise.
- **Noise Monitor** - uses a nonverbal signal to remind group members to quiet down.
- **Energizer** - energizes the group when motivation is low by suggesting ideas through humor or by being enthusiastic.
- **Reporter** - reports the group's finding to the class.

Learning Outcomes

In Leikin and Zaslavsky's study (1997), students' learning in traditional setting was compared with their learning by the exchange-of-knowledge method. The finding in this study shows that the experimental small–group cooperative learning setting facilitates a higher level of learning activities. Listed in the chart below is an average amount of student retention, transfer, and application of knowledge. This research is based upon eleven years of research that asks the questions, "What causes learning in the classroom?" Listed below is a chart depicting the percentage of learning retention, transfer, and application of how best a student learns information through a myriad of modalities.

Consequence: Average Amount of Retention, Transfer, and Application	
Lecture	5%
Reading	10%
Audio – Visual	20%
Demonstration	30%
Discussion Group	50%
Practice "Real World" Applications	70%
Teach Others/Immediate Use of Learning	90%

Salmon River – GLC Eisenhower Project

MAKING COOPERATIVE LEARNING WORK

According to Stahl & Vansickle (1987), educators need to learn the essential elements of cooperative learning for at least two reasons. First, they need to tailor cooperative learning to their unique instructional needs, circumstances, curricula, subject areas, and students. Secondly, instructors must have the students working together in cohesive groups. These groups will be checked occasionally through the intervening process for stability and understanding. This process will help enhance the effectiveness of the student learning groups. For the effectiveness of cooperative learning, teachers must understand the essential elements of cooperation if they are to implement cooperative learning successfully.

Stahl & Vansickle (1987) further go on to say that when teachers have real expertise in using cooperative learning, they will structure five essential elements into instructional activities. The researchers also say that well–structured and poorly structured cooperative learning lessons in the classroom at all levels can be distinguished on the basis of these elements. These essential elements, furthermore, should be carefully structured within all levels of cooperative efforts. To make cooperative learning strategies work, teachers must have present these essentials of cooperative learning strategies, which are as follows:

1. Positive interdependence
2. Face–to–face promotional and positive interaction
3. Individual accountability
4. Social skills
5. Group processing

Researchers have noted that through the attainment of conceptual understanding of how to teach, true teaching genius can emerge and be expressed. Once teachers understand and learn the essential elements of cooperative learning strategies, they can fine-tune and adapt them to their specific circumstances, needs, and students.

ALTERNATIVE APPROACHES TO COOPERATIVE LEARNING

According to Stahl & Vansickle (1987), there are five alternative approaches to implementing cooperative learning strategies: direct approaches, lesson approach, strategy approach, curriculum package approach, and cooperative activities approach.

Stahl & Vansickle (1987) state that the direct approaches to cooperative learning are relatively inexpensive and take little time to implement. This allows teachers to use a specific cooperative learning lesson, curriculum, or strategy. These direct applications are basically theoretical. The goal is to train teachers to use step–by- step, prescribed procedures and curriculum materials that teachers have used successfully in the classroom. This approach allows the trainer to inform the trainees about the procedure and to demonstrate it on models; then the trainees practice the procedure. Furthermore, teachers must keep in mind that the direct approach focuses on specific lessons, strategies, and curriculums.

Stahl & Vansickle (1987) go on to say that another approach is the Lesson Approach. This approach allows for teachers to be trained in how to use cooperative learning strategies. Teachers are given a specific lesson structured cooperatively (such as an English lesson on punctuation, a mathematical lesson on long division, or a science lesson on what sinks and what floats), and they are shown a demonstration of how the lesson is taught. From this approach teachers are then expected to go back to their classrooms and conduct the lesson.

A third approach suggested by Stahl & Vansickle (1987) trains teachers to use specific cooperative learning strategies, typically demonstrated with one or more specific lessons. Once teachers learn the strategy, it may be used to build a number of cooperative lessons and integrate them into existing curriculums. Some of the most powerful strategies include the Jigsaw method developed by Elliot Aronson and his colleagues (1978), the Co–op Co–op strategy refined by Spencer Kagan (1988), the Group Project method developed by Sharan and Sharan (1976), and Math Groups–of–Four developed by Marilyn Burns (1981).

A fourth approach is the curriculum package approach, which trains teachers to use a curriculum package within which lessons are structured cooperatively. Through this approach teachers are given a preset curriculum that contains all the materials and procedures necessary for implementation in the classroom and are told how to use these learning strategies in the classroom. As with all curriculums, the packages tend to be subject area and grade level specific. Dozens of curriculum packages are being published that include instructions for using cooperative learning groups with the lessons.

And finally, the fifth approach is the cooperative activities that are related to cooperative learning in the classroom. Teachers may use group building activities such as favorite sports and hobbies, pets I wish I had, team juggling, and cooperative games.

These approaches are most effective when there is a required combination of a conceptual understanding of the essential elements of cooperative learning, concrete examples of lessons and strategies, opportunities for practice with feedback, and implementation over on extended period of time in the classroom.

GUIDELINES FOR
ABILITY GROUPING

According to Stahl & Vansickle (1987), the cooperative groups should model democratic values and should be characterized by shared responsibility, interdependence, the value of the individual, and equality of educational opportunity. The researchers further go on to say that developing basic citizenship skills and getting a good education helps to encourage students to work with others from different backgrounds which promote the concept of democracy. Researchers continue to state that through shared values students are aided in developing good effective learning skills as well as enhanced educational opportunities that elevate students to achieve higher levels of knowledge with other learners with different values and methods all while working in a heterogeneous grouping environment like one would find in a democracy. These purposes are incongruous with homogeneous grouping.

Stahl & Vansickle (1987) encourage educators to support heterogeneous grouping in the classroom and to work to foster appropriate learning strategies suited to effective instructions in such groups.

COOPERATIVE LEARNING ACTIVITIES

Introduction

The cooperative learning strategy promotes an environment that encourages students to become actively involved in the learning process. Research has shown that this learning method allows the learner to show an understanding of the importance of hard work, continuous learning, sharing of ideas, and it also helps to construct independent thinking skills that lead to an effective life- long learning. These cooperative learning activities emphasize varied experiences in problem solving, such as how to investigate content, develop strategies, interpret results, and, finally, be able to generalize solutions in a meaningful way.

Therefore, as the groups begin to develop various strategies and begin to share expertise or show a need for more direction, it is still the teacher who is walking around the room, who is looking, listening, and offering guidance. Finally, it is the instructor who must monitor each student's strengths and weaknesses through all of this inter-group interaction.

Write a Postcard

Curriculum: Social Studies
Objective: Select information
Material: Reference books, unlined 3 x 5" cards, pen or pencil
Time: Approximately 40 minutes
Suggested Grouping: Cooperative grouping
Teacher Guidance: Low
Outside Research: High

Advance Preparation: You will need encyclopedias or travel guidebooks.

Activity: Students learn about a foreign country and write postcards describing one of its attractions.

Connection: Review the writing process and writing picture postcards. Ask students to think about a foreign country that they would like to visit.

Make new discoveries: Each group chooses a foreign country the members would like to visit. They use books to gather information about that country. Each student picks a different place or attraction in his or her group's country, researches it, and then writes a postcard about a visit to that place.

Role-Play A TV Interview

Curriculum: Speaking
Objective: Speak on a given topic
Materials: Stage props such as chairs and microphones, TV camera, cue cards
Time: About 45 minutes
Suggested grouping: Cooperative groups

Activity: Invite students to role–play the Today Show in which Vicki Van Meter is interviewing ED by Bryant Gumbel.

Guide: Students are to write a script focusing on additional questions. Clarify. All group members should collaborate on the script. While one student acts as recorder, others might take turns role–playing Vicki and Gumbel. Other group members can create cue cards.

Encourage: Team members are to share responsibilities for the presentation. Members can perform the various jobs of a TV studio crew. After rehearsing the talk show interview, encourage the team to present it to the class.

Mini–Lesson

Teach/Model: Remind students that preparation for an interview is very important. Questions need to focus on a specific topic or topics and be planned and organized in a logical sequence so that one question leads naturally to the next.

Apply: Encourage teams to brainstorm questions they would like to discuss with Vicki. Then have them narrow the questions down under one organizing topic for the interview.

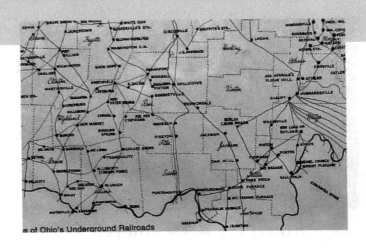

s of Ohio's Underground Railroads

Walk Across History

Curriculum Focus: Math
Objective: Break a problem into small parts
Materials: Paper, pencil, and a map of Ohio
Time: About 30 minutes
Suggested Grouping: Cooperative Grouping
Teacher Guidance: Low
Outside Research: None

Advance Preparation: You'll need an atlas or encyclopedia with a map of Ohio.

Activity: Students estimate how many days it would take them to travel across Ohio on foot.

Connection: Shows how slaves escaped across Ohio form south to north.

Make New Discoveries: Students use a map of Ohio to find out how far they'd have to walk. They estimate how far they could walk in a day. Encourage students to use their experience to reach this figure. Groups demonstrate how they arrived at their answers.

How to Assess: Were students able to arrive at a reasonable answer and demonstrate how they made their calculations? Were students able accurately to represent numerical data on a bar graph?

Graph Immigration

Curriculum Focus: Social Studies
Objective: Use carts, graphs, and visual displays.
Materials: Reference materials, paper, pencils, poster board, and markers.
Time: About 40 minutes
Suggested Grouping: Cooperative groupings.
Teacher Guidance: Low
Outside Research: Moderate

Advance Preparation: Graph reference sources that contain immigration information such as The World Book encyclopedia or an almanac.

Activity: Students make a bar graph comparing the number of immigrants admitted into the United States from 1870 through 1980.

Connection: Read in an encyclopedia about where immigrants settled at the turn of the century. Ask students why cities offered immigrants the best chances for jobs.

Make New Discoveries: Groups find lists of immigration figures and plan how to turn them into a bar graph. They decide what each axis of their graph will represent. Students produce their graphs of immigration figures on poster board.

Find Forensic Evidence

Curriculum Focus: Science
Objective: Use observation
Time: About 30 minutes
Suggested Grouping: Cooperative groups

Activity: Students mark out a small area inside the school and examine it for forensic evidence.

Connection: Discuss the different things that can be used as forensic evidence.

Make New Discoveries: Have them examine the area closely. Students can keep track of what they find by writing detailed descriptions or making drawings. Students can then use the evidence to make hypotheses. For instance: There's been a lot of rain; people have come in without wiping their shoes.

How to Assess: Were students able to gather forensic evidence and use it to form hypotheses?

Forensic Criminologist Lab

Curriculum Focus: Science
Objective: Use Observation
Time: About 30 minutes
Suggested Grouping: Cooperative groups

Activity: Students fingerprint their classmates. Next, they will use the prints a mystery.

Make New Discoveries: Encourage students to develop a filing system for their fingerprints.

How to Assess: Were students able to make clear fingerprints and use them to compile a fingerprint file?

Team Recognition

Main idea: Figure individual improvement scores and team scores and award certificates or other team awards.

- Award teams or individual awards for successful completion of the skill learned.
- Improvement points
- Students earn points recording the quiz scores:

Quiz	Improvement Points
More than 10 points below base score	0
Base score 10 points	10
Base score to 10 points above base score	20
More than 10 points above abase score	30
Perfect paper (regardless of base score)	40

Time: One class period
Main Idea: Individual quiz
Material needed:
- One quiz per student
- Administer quiz. Allot time to complete the quiz. Taking a quiz is an individualized activity and is not to be shared.
- Use a variety of methods to score quizzes. Examples, exchange papers with members of other teams or collect for checking.

Team Work in STAD
(Student Teams Achievement Divisions)

On the first day of team work in STAD, you should explain to students what it means to work in teams. Before beginning the process, discuss the following team rules:

1) Students will be responsible for making sure that each teammate is knowledgeable about the material taught.
2) All team members must complete the required work before any member is finished.
3) Students must ask their teammates questions before asking the teacher.

Teams are encouraged to add additional rules if necessary and then proceed as follows:

- Teams are to move three desks together or move to team tables.
- Allot time to choose a team name.
- Administer worksheets and answer sheets (two for each team).
- Have students reduce team size as necessary.
- All teammates are required to study until all students are knowledgeable about the subject and score 100% on the quiz.
- Circulate throughout the teams, praising, sitting in team discussions, and so on.

Test

- Maintain momentum by eliminating interruptions, asking many questions, and moving rapidly throughout the lesson.

Guided Practice

- Have students work problems or examples or prepare answers to your questions.
- Call on students at random. Allow for students to prepare for correct answers.
- Do not give long class assignments but have the students work one or two problems or examples or prepare one or two answers, then give feedback.

Team Study

Time: 1–2 class periods.
Main idea: Students study worksheets in their teams.
Materials needed: Issue two worksheets for every team. Have two answer sheets for each team.

- During team study, have each team member perform a task to master the material that is presented.
- During this process teams are to help each other master or learn the material. Students should have worksheets and answer sheets; they can practice the skill being taught while assessing the performance of each team member.
- Administer two worksheets per team, thus forcing teams to work together. Each lesson in STAD begins with a class presentation. The presentation should cover the opening, development, and guided practice components of your total lesson; the team activities and quiz cover independent practice and assessment, respectively. Remember to stress in your lesson, the following:

Open
- Tell students what they are about to learn and why it is important. Arouse students' curiosity with a puzzling demonstration, real–life problem, or other means.
- Briefly review any prerequisite skills or information.

Development

- Stick close to the objectives that you will test.
- Focus on meaning, not memorization.
- Actively demonstrate concepts or skills, using visual aids, manipulatives, and any other examples.
- Frequently assess student comprehension by asking many questions.
- Explain why an answer is correct or incorrect, unless this is obvious.
- Move rapidly to the next concept as soon as students have grasped the main idea.

Example of an Average of Three Test Scores

Sara's	90
	84
	87
	261 / 3 = 87
Sara's Base Score =	87

STAD
(Student Teams Achievement Divisions)

Regular Cycle of Instruction

Teach: Present the lesson!
Team Study: Students work on worksheets in
their teams to master the material.
Test: Students take individual quizzes.
Team recognition: Compute team scores based on team members'
improvement scores. Individual certificates, a class newsletter, or a bulletin
board recognize high–scoring teams.

STAD Activities in Detail

Teach: Present the lesson!
Time: 1–2 class periods
Main idea: Present the lesson.
Material needed: Your lesson plan. You should change team assignments
by trading students of the same appropriate performance level but of
different ethnicity or sex among teams until a balance is achieved.
Fill out team summary sheets: Have the students fill in their names on
each team summary sheet, leaving the team name space blank.

Report on Cowboy Tall Tales

Subject: Writing/Speaking
Introduce the activity by discussing tall tales about western heroes and cowboys. Talk about bigger–than–life characters with whom they may be familiar, such as Paul Bunyan, Sally Ann Thunder, and Davy Crockett.
Material: Pecos Bill tall–tale books (e.g., Pecos Bill by Ariane Dewey, American Tall Tales by Adrian Stoutenberg)
Time: About 30 minutes
Suggested Grouping: Cooperative groups

Encourage students to read a cowboy tall tale from the library. Have them make notes about the plot, setting, and characters as they read. Have students write a book report on the tall tale, including a description of the plot and why they would not recommend the book to others. They might also want to compare what happens in the story to the actual facts about cowboys as explained in the selection.

Mini–Lesson
Teach/Model: Remind students that a book report can contain a brief summary of the plot or main idea of the text as well as a description of the characters and setting. In addition, a report often describes whether the book is recommended or not and why. Point out that there are other ways students can share books – shoebox movies, original book covers, authored letters, dioramas, and dramatizations.

Apply: Have students write a brief book report on the tall tale they checked out of the library.

COOPERATIVE LEARNING RESOURCES

Recommended Literature List

Cooperative Learning in Mathematics: Handbook for Teachers, Davidson, N., Editor, Addison Wesley, 1990.

National Council of Teachers of Mathematics, Curriculum and Evaluation Standards.

National Council of Teacher of Mathematics Professional Standards. Get it together: Math Problems for Groups, Grades 4 – 12, EQUAL, Lawrence Hall of Science. Berkeley, CA.

Assessment Alternatives in Mathematics, EQEALS, Lawrence Hall of Science, Berkeley, CA, 1989.

Designing Group work: Strategies for the Heterogeneous Classroom, 2nd Edition, Cohen, E., 1994.

Cooperative Learning: The Magazine for Cooperation in Education, (The magazine is sent to all members of IASCE.)

Cooperative Learning to Support Thinking, Reasoning, and Communication in Mathematics, Roberston, L., Davidson, N., and Dees, R., Chapter in Handbook of Cooperative Learning Methods, Sharan, S., Editor, Greenwood Publishers, 1994.

Circles of Learning. Cooperation in the Classroom, (4th ed) Johnson, D., Johnson, R., and Johnson Holubec, E., Interaction Book Company, Edina, MN, 1993.

Joining Together. Group Theory and Skills, Johnson, W. and Johnson, F., Allyn and Bacon, 1994.

No Contest: The Case Against Competition, Kohn, and Alfie, Houghton Mifflin Company, 1986.

The Cooperative Sports and Games Book: Challenge without Competition, Orlick, T., Pantheon Books, Nym 1978.

The Second Cooperative Sports and Games Book, Orlick, T., Pantheon Books, NY, 1982.

Animal Town: Cooperative Ventures.

Enhancing thinking through cooperative learning, Davidson, N., and Worsham, T., Editors, Teachers College Press, New York, 1992.

Expanding cooperative learning through group investigation, Sharan, Y. and Sharan, S., Teachers College Press, New York, 1992.

SUMMARY

This guide benefits learners of all ages and academic levels. Cooperative learning has proven to be an effective teaching method for teachers regardless of the intellectual level of the students. Therefore, this chapter introduced the teachers to the following three areas: conceptual viewpoint, how to implement the process, and suggested strategies, resources, and activities needed for success.

REFERENCES

Aronsom, Elliot. (2000). Jigsaw classroom. <u>Social Psychology Network</u>.

Bassett, c. 7 & McWhiter, J. J. & Kitzmiller, K. (1999). Teacher implementation of cooperative learning groups. <u>Contemporary Education</u>, 71, 46.

Brandt, R. S. & Meek, A. (1990). Cooperative learning. <u>Educational Leadership</u>, vol. 3, 47.

Chun-Yen Chang & Song-Ling Mao, (November, 1999). The effects on student's cognitive achievement when using the cooperative learning method in earth science classroom. <u>School Science & Mathematics</u>, 99, 374.

Forte, I., Schurr, S. (1994). <u>Interdisciplinary Units And Projects for Thematic Instruction for the Middle Grade Success</u>. Nashville, TN: Incentive Publication, Inc., 46.

Fullan, J.G., Bennett, B., & Rolheiser-Bennett, C. (1990). Linking classroom and school improvement. <u>Educational Leadership</u>, 47, 13-19.

Gillies, R. M. & Ashman, A. F. (2000). The effect of cooperative learning on students with learning difficulties in the lower elementary school. <u>Journal of Special Education</u>, vol. 4, 19.

Johnson, D. W. & Johnson, R. T. (1999). Making cooperative learning work. <u>Theory into Practice</u>, 7, 38, 67.

King, J. R. (December, 2000). Cooperative learning in context/ particularities: Book Review. <u>Journal of Contemporary Ethnography</u>, 7, 6, 9, 29, 747.

Leikin, R., Zaslavsky, O. (1999). Cooperative learning in mathematics. <u>The Mathematics Teacher</u>, 92, 240-246.

Melser, N. A. (May/June, 1999). Gifted students and cooperative learning: A study of grouping strategies. <u>Roper Review</u>, p. 315.

O'Donnell, A. M. & Dansereeau, D. F. (2000). Interactive effects of prior knowledge and material format on cooperative learning. <u>Journal of Experimental Education</u>, 68, 101.

Onwuegbuzie, A. J. (January/February, 2001). Relationship between peer orientation and achievement in cooperative learning - based research. <u>Journal of Educational research</u>, 94, 156.

Prater, M. A. & Bruhl, S. (May/June, 1998). Acquiring social skills through cooperative learning and teacher directed instruction. <u>Remedial & Special Education</u>, 19, 160.

Randall, V. (March/April, 1999). Cooperative learning: abused and overused. <u>Gifted Child Today</u>, 14 - 16. Operative learning and the academically talented students. <u>The National Research on the Gifted and Talented</u>.

Salmon River - GLC Eisenhower Project.

Salvin, R. E. (1999). Comprehensive approaches to cooperative learning. <u>Theory into Practice</u>, 38, 74.

Stahl, R. & Vansickle, R. L. (1987). <u>Cooperative Learning In the Social Studies Classroom: An Introduction to Social Study</u>. NCSS Publication: Washington, DC.

Salvin, R. E. (October, 1995). <u>Research on Cooperative Learning And Achievement: What We Know, What We Need to Know</u>. Scholastic – Literacy Place Reading.

Sharan, S., & Shachar, H. (1988). <u>Language and learning in the cooperative classroom</u>. New York: Springer Verlag.

Siciliano, J. I. (2001). How to incorporate cooperative learning principles in the classroom: it's more than just putting students in teams. <u>Journal of Management Education</u>, 25, 8-20.

Stearns, C. J. (1999). A middle school venture into cooperative learning: Successes and dilemmas. <u>Theory Into Practice</u>, 38, 100.

Storm, R. D. & Strom, P. S. (April/May, 1998). Student participation in the evaluation of cooperative learning. <u>Community College Journal of Research, and Practice</u>, 22, 265.

Webb, N. M. (1989). Peer interaction and learning in small groups. <u>International Review of Educational Research</u>, 13, 21-40.

EVALUATION FORM

Please take a few minutes to complete the following evaluation form.

On a scale of 1 - 5, please circle the relevant response for each question.
5= very useful   4=useful
3=fairly useful   2=not useful   1=No opinion

1. How useful was this guide in understanding the cooperative learning concept?	5 4 3 2 1
2. How useful was the guide in helping you to implement cooperative learning strategies?	5 4 3 2 1
3. How useful were the strategies and activities presented in helping students to achieve?	5 4 3 2 1
4. Would you recommend this guide to others in the educational field to use?	*Circle one:* YES NO Not Sure (explain below)
Thank you!	

Please forward all compliments, comments, and constructive criticisms to:
Mrs. June Veasley
P.O. Box 371645, Decatur, Georgia 30037
Email: junebelcherveasley@gmail.com

CHAPTER IV
RECOMMENDATIONS AND CONCLUSION

*In an industrial organization, it's the group effort
that counts. There is really no room for stars in an industrial
organization. You need talented people, but they can't do it alone.
They have to have help.*

~John F. Donnelly, President, Donnelly Mirrors, 2003

SUMMARY

In summary, cooperative learning has been a viable teaching strategy in the elementary classroom for many years. Teachers in classrooms have used it across the United States and across the curriculum for many years. Such methods benefited the teacher and learner more than other teaching methods. Teachers and learners benefited from the implementation of the cooperative learning models because they integrated the essential elements of positive interdependence, face-to-face interaction, individual accountability, social skills, and group processes that are vital to the learner. Teachers have tailored cooperative learning methods to specifically address their personal, school, class, subject, and student circumstances and needs (Stahl, VanSickle, 1987).

RECOMMENDATION

It is recommended that teachers use this handbook to help foster the grouping method and the academic success of elementary age learners. Teachers are to keep in mind that cooperative learning is a complex instructional procedure that requires conceptual knowledge as well as the skills of using specific lessons, curricula, and strategies. If cooperative learning is going to be institutionalized, classroom teachers must become experts on the conceptual system of understanding how cooperative lessons should be structured to obtain the maximum learning benefit possible. Additionally, teachers must know how the problems associated with adapting cooperative learning strategies/methods to the specific learning of students can be overcome.

Finally, teachers must keep in mind that there are no quick solutions or shortcuts to becoming an effective cooperative learning facilitator. They must be willing to become life-long learners so that the expertise needed to implement cooperative learning effectively is perfected and passed on to new stakeholders. (Stahl, Vansickle, 1987).

CONCLUSION

In conclusion, research has proven that students learn more effectively when they work cooperatively than when they work individually or competitively (Salvin & Johnson, 2000). Students who work cooperatively have a higher success rate academically and are more positive about school and teachers when they work in cooperative learning groups. They become more tolerant of each other regardless of ability, ethnic background, or handicap when they work in cooperative groups. It has been proven that when the cooperative learning concept is used effectively, students are more positive about taking part in the following:

- Discussions
- Display better interaction skills
- Develop high self-esteem
- Establish high expectation about working with others cooperatively.

In addition, utilizing the cooperative learning method, many teachers will find that it not only builds students' academic achievement, but teachers are able to manage hands-on activities in the classroom effectively. Teachers must also keep in mind that when the cooperative learning method is implemented correctly, the following things take place:

- Activity is a student-focused event.
- Students, not the teacher, manage the material.
- Teachers have more time to disseminate and facilitate the lesson.
- Responsibility for learning the concepts are taught.
- There is alleviation of some of the stress that builds up when trying to maintain order and keep students on task.

P.O. Box 453
Powder Springs, Georgia 30127
www.entegritypublishing.com
info@entegritypublishing.com
770.727.6517

CPSIA information can be obtained
at www.ICGtesting.com
Printed in the USA
LVHW062141160520
655784LV00004B/193

9 781732 576780